FIRST DAY OF SCHOOL
Do You Want To Be My Friend?

by Jennifer Bisram

illustrated by Generlyn Jean & Lloydlyn Jean

Bizzy Books Publishing

This book belongs to

_____

Published by Bizzy Books Publishing.
Copyright © 2014 Jennifer Bisram

All rights reserved. No part of this publication may be reproduced, stored in a retrieval system, or transmitted, in any form or by any means, electronic, mechanical, photocopying, recording, or otherwise, without prior written permission from the publisher.

Questions or comments?
Write to:
Bizzy Books Publishing
P.O. BOX 421724
Kissimmee, FL 34741

Email:
info@bizzybookspublishing.com

Visit:
www.bizzybookspublishing.com

Library of Congress Control Number: 2014913868
ISBN 978-0-692-25519-3
Manufactured in the United States of America.

This book was inspired by my sister, who was not afraid to make new friends on her first day of school.

-Jennifer Bisram

Hi, my name is Star. Do you want to be my friend?

Okay, my name is Anjali. I am from India, where the Taj Mahal is located. My favorite foods are roti and curry. My mom wears a red dot on her forehead to show she is married.

My name is Tony. I am from Italy. Our capital is Rome. Do you know the Pope lives there? I like to eat pizza and pasta.

And my name is Jin. I am from China. My mom says it is the birthplace of tea. My dad says the Chinese invented paper and kites. He eats everything with chopsticks!

Hi, my name is Kwame. And my name is Abena. We are from Africa, where the largest desert in the world is located. It is called the Sahara Desert. Do you know the largest living land animal also lives there? It is the African Elephant.

Hello, I am Simon. My family is from Belgium. They say it is world famous for chocolate and waffles.

Hi. My name is Star. Do you want to be my friend?

Surely. I am Danica from Poland where people say the biggest section in most grocery stores there is the candy aisle!

And my name is Donovan. I am from the Caribbean Island of Jamaica, the birthplace of Bob Marley and reggae music. My favorite food there is jerk chicken. Did you know the Caribbean has more than 25 island nations and thousands of individual islands? Look at the map!

Hi my name is Star. Do you want to be my friend?

Sure. My name is Kanya. I am from Thailand, where the world's largest gold Buddha statue is located. Did you know rain falls almost every day in May, June, July, August and September in Thailand too?

And I am Emma from Australia. My parents say koalas, kangaroos and platypuses live there. Did you know Australia has more reptile species than any other country in the world?

Hi. My name is Senta. I am from Germany, where Albert Einstein was born. I heard Germans invented gummy bears. Oh, and we have over 300 kinds of bread in Germany.

And I am Javier from Honduras. Every year on September 10th, we celebrate Honduras Day of the Child.

My name is Beatriz. My family is from Ecuador, where that banana you are eating may have come from. My grandma says many of the world's bananas are grown in Ecuador.

And I am Lolita from Spain. My papa makes traditional dishes from there like paella, a type of rice dish. And, at the dinner table we always have tapas, which is a range of small snacks.

Hi, my name is Star. Do you want to be my friend?

Yes. My name is Abrahem. I am from Israel where the Western Wall is located. My mom packs me traditional snacks from there all the time, like this bamba.

And my name is Akila. I am from Egypt where the longest river in the world runs through. It is called the Nile.

I am Irvin from Scotland. My grandpa says Scotland has over 300 railway stations. Did you know the bagpipe is considered Scotland's national instrument and is one of the most iconic symbols of Scottish culture? Oh, and kilts are traditional clothing worn by many men there.

I am Zara from Malaysia where the Petronas Towers, two of the tallest twin buildings in the world are located. My dad says Malaysians like to make artwork like carved wooden masks and handwoven baskets.

And my name is Nazli. I am from Turkey, where my grandpa says lots of cars and planes are made. My favorite food there is kebab and lokum.

I am Florine from France. The Eiffel Tower is in Paris, France. It is one of the most visited monuments in the world.

I am Camilo from Colombia where there are lots of emeralds. My mom says we supply businesses around the world with the stones.

And I am Habiba from Saudi Arabia. We have two of the holiest places of Islam there. They are Mecca and Medina.

I am Prakash. My family is from Guyana, where Kaieteur Falls is located. My dad says it is one of the most powerful waterfalls in the world. Did you know people from around the world go there for gold because it has one of the largest gold mines in South America too?

Don't forget about me! I am Akiko from Japan. People say it is one of the largest automobile makers in the world.

And I am Jasmine. My family is from Canada, where there are over 30,000 lakes. Many people there speak English and French and play Hockey, like my brother Jonathan.

Hi, my name is Star. Do you want to be my friend?

Okay. My name is Katia. I was born in Russia. My uncle says it is one of the largest countries in the world. Did you know it is believed to be bigger than the planet Pluto?

Hello, my name is Star. Do you want to be my friend?

Of course. I am Ciara. I am from Ireland where Saint Patrick's Day is a national holiday. It is also celebrated in many places around the world. Did you know the shamrock is our national symbol? Many people believe it brings them luck.

And, I am Zenobia. I am from Greece where there are more than a hundred million olive trees. My dad says the country produces most of the world's black olives. Did you know Greeks wave with a closed hand because it is considered an insult to show the palm of the hand with fingers extended?

Hi, my name is Star. Can I sit next to you? Do you want to be my friend?

Gladly. My name is Hertha. I am from England where Buckingham Palace is located. It is where the Queen lives. My sister says it is so big it has its own police station. Did you know that the first hot chocolate store opened in London, England?

And my name is Natalia. I am from Chile where the Atacama Desert is located. My cousin says it is one of the driest areas on Earth. I hear Chile is the top grower of grapes.

Hi, I am Finn. My family is from Norway, the Land of the Midnight Sun. It is called that because during the summer months the sun never sets. The sun is still up at night, even when it is my bedtime!

And I am Eduardo from Brazil. My mom says The Statue of Christ the Redeemer, which is located on the top of the Corcovado Mountain, is considered one of the new seven wonders of the world. She says it is one of the tallest religious statues in the world too.

Hi, my name is Star. Do you want to be my friend?

Certainly. My name is Freba. My family is from Afghanistan, a country rich in natural gas and oil. My mom says many people there grow and sell crops, like vegetables, fruits and rice for a living. They like to read poetry and fly kites too!

And my name is Yolanda. My family is from Mexico, one of the most populated countries in the world. Did you know the red poinsettia flower originated from Mexico? My aunt always makes me tacos, burritos and enchiladas that she learned to make there.

Hello. My name is Star. Do you want to be my friend?

Sure. My name is Yejun. My family is from South Korea. My mom says many stores there stay open overnight for people to shop!

Hi. My name is Star. Do you want to be my friend?

Okay. My name is Alfonso. My family is from Costa Rica. My grandpa says more than 1,000 kinds of butterflies live there.

Hi, my name is Star. Do you want to be my friend?

Alright. My name is Ahmed. My family is from Morocco. Moroccans are known for many handcrafts such as handwoven wool carpets and hand-painted ceramics. Did you know people there often touch the right hand to the heart as a sign of respect?

I am Gustavo from Bolivia, one of the wettest zones on the planet because of all of the rainfall every year. My mom says the largest deposit of salt on the planet is found in Bolivia too.

My name is Pala. My family is from Iceland. My grandma says it is covered by ice, glaciers and geysers and has more than 20 active volcanoes. My family's favorite snack there is cocoa soup, which is like hot chocolate, but thicker.

And I am Olga from Finland, the country of a thousand lakes and islands. Did you know it has more than 180,000 lakes and nearly 180,000 islands? My mom says my cousins who live there do not start school until they are seven years-old.

Do you want to know my name? It is Wapasha. My family is Native American. We are made up of lots of tribes, live all over America and are often called Indians. Did you know every tribe has its own tribal clothes and headdresses?